Layered Longings

Collected Poems

MARSHALL COOMBS

ISBN 978-1-3999—0865-8

Published by Orinoco Publishing

Printed in Great Britain by
White Hart Press Ltd
Bedford

ORINOCO PUBLISHING

June

I hope some of these poems
resonate for you.
Warmest good wishes
Marshall
December 2022

For Roger, my family and all my friends

CONTENTS

7. The Humming
8. The Opals of Fantasy
9. The Lawn
10. April
11. September Sunlight
12. A Winter Ceilidh
13. Morris Dance
14. Hastings by Angielight
15. Winterjack
16. Festival family
18. A Welter of Days – A Lull in March
19. When My Children are Asleep
20. Dark Mercy
21. Dreams Lie Dustlly
22. Thirty
23. The War
24. Desert and Courtyard
25. Qanawat Temple
26. A Nile Journey
27. The Spice that is Morocco
28. Seeing Through
30. Dream and Daylight
31. Paper Boat
32. Sleep
33. Mousediary : Midwinter
34. Steeple Woods
35. Emma, sheep dog
36. Lawn, Normandy, June
38. Coltsfoot
39. Isle of Mull
40. The Wind in the Long Grass
41. Seadream
42. Sylvia Plath
43. August

44. Capri
46. Cyclades Days – Breakfast
47. Morning
48. Midday
49. Afternoon
50. Evening
52. Elderflower Champagne
54. High Summer
55. The World for his Pleasure
56. Landscape, Seascape
57. At Seventy
58. Mahé, Seychelles

The Humming

A deep, old lane,
muddy. May. On the banks
hawthorns, scabby brown trunks
muscling up through the yellow green
of the baby-fingered leaves
filtering sun. Promise of summer shadows.
Boys in the lane
mudlarking, laughing
then between their shouts

hum tremble zing! hush

the deep vibration of a multitude;
suddenly I knew: overhead
a white dome
of sweetcoarse mayflowers,
thousands, nectared
by whole hives of bees.

Boys,sh! ...and beyond
the imperial hum-zing
a cuckoo sounded

melodious thrumming quaking quiet

and the sky came down
to the speedwell at our feet
shaking the lane, the mud, our laughter

in that humming of heaven.

The Opals of Fantasy

There was dirt beneath his fingernails.

Or: he has been deep in the domain of Logres
and the loam of legend has imbued his hands.

Try again: after gardening, she brewed the tea.

Or: out of the grey wastes of exhaustion and worldstain
she came, bearing the elixir of friendship and refreshment.

Fantasy just doesn't work for me, you said.

In my eyes, the cold salt water of reality
comes alive in the shimmering sunlight:

the opals of fantasy elucidate the blind brown rock.

The Lawn

Driving to work
through brown winter flatlands
mind half hurrying, radio on.

Sudden rightangle, as if some old farmer
stood at the corner with folded arms –
not across my land! –
and here's his scruffy working yard
big machines idle, chaffing each other.

Next corner, neat cottage
a triangular tree
and a perfect square of dew:
a lawn, silk fur
untouched by season
primary sunlit green.

You're bustling on, but your mind curves back
through layered longings to the quiet lawn,
the set-apart place you've always wanted –
the quick welcome of it! –
the you-yourself place, awake, alive

waiting for lovers.

April
(for Marian Mason and the Old Town Singers)

Winter lingers on and on,
brown on brown, decay and grime;
dreams of spring are gone, are gone,
no new once upon a time.

One grey morning there's a bird
like a bellows, wheezing, ringing
and the April sun has heard
rising, sparkling and singing –

Out of the house and breathe the breeze!
In zig-zags below, and fluttering high
come flower-fumbling bumblebees,
the tumbling first blue butterfly.

September Sunlight

When the clear and golden early autumn light
streams over the East Hill, it suffuses
the cool mist in the Old Town Valley
with a gentle blue, and the hurrushing
off-to-work traffic is only a rustle
on the surface of the stillness of the morning.

Then my heart stirs, troubled by wonder.
As if the light remembers summer
and makes me think how far I have come
so far, what I have done, and look
back to my old home, the making home,
and forward, home, with the clear light shining.

Light like a rich Book of Hours
not sharp as Spring, but a light
under an eternal eye, my life
illuminated without accusation
but with a coolth; some falling away.
Time to move on...

a light of meeting and acknowledgement
which I have known before, and will again
perhaps, after my dissolution, as I sense
this is the light of the essential.
The air is full of beams and shadows.
Time to move on...

A Winter Ceilidh

As we drove to the ceilidh
Orion flickered and flashed
the stars themselves
dancing crystals of frost
the moon an axe-edge of icefire.

Outside the hall
the music sounded
hurdy-gurdy, merry within.
We hurried to join, night's grip
black, pressing, penetrating.

Confusion of feet
and social awkwardness
bobychill resistant to the music
the cave of the stomach
reverberating.

A simple bourrée, drum and corm
a village sound, and feet
start, stepping gently
body thawing, now pulsating
fire to the fingers, fire to the toes –

and that should be the climax
the movement swirling care away
a centrifugal force:
we're the world, the world's a dance!
I call, longing to be there

but this winter night
there is a crystal of self
that stays with the cold stars, watching:
there are distances
other patterns than yours, dancer.

A Morris Dance
(to the tune of Sweet Jenny Jones)

Clump on the base note and
  donk the arpeggio
    village hall pianist
      plays morris tunes.

"Sweet Jenny Jones"
  from the village of Adderb'ry
    lives in the feet
      tracing motifs like runes.

Her time may be cobwebbed
  but in memory, visiting
    perfectly flowers
      the old country scene.

Rural folk then
  had their pain and their hardships;
    the current of time
      blent their dance with routine.

What we remember is
  patterned endurance,
    like samplers embroidered
      in faded silk thread.

Momently, dancers from
  nearby suburbia
    open the door
      between living and dead.

Hastings by Angielight
(for Angela Braven: painting "Tropical Hastings")

My common-or-garden's never been the same.
She's witched and rainbowed it, with her raven hair
and tropical palette. A blushing flame

pulses its pale Englishness. Now, when the fair
and dog-rosed summer blooms, my granny's bonnets
are embravened. Autumn's cool and misty air

flushes with sunset fantasies from its
African memories. Even the brown leaves curl
for bright-edged words, aspire to sonnets.

November cold, and Hastings greys, sea pearl,
fluoresce in Angie's canvases. Their inward
colours, caught at sunmagnitude, swirl

and flourish. Her paintprophesies overheard,
they rapturously await the humming bird.

Winterjack
(Jack-in-the-Green's February thoughts)

sleepydayseeings

leafmouldearth
shrivelsloe barkbound
rainysky
fernslowthoughtsgrow

sunbreak
rootcool hrrmmm
hmm branchwarm

ohdreamscome
budburst leavesthrust
flowercrownpetalstream
jackmusic jackdances

sapsurgefountain
emeraldscatter

everywheregreen
nowherejack

gruffwinter
kernelkeep
greengarner
dreamsleep

Folk Festival Family

Old friends gather
for a gossip outside the marquee
with a welcome beer
(and a bacon sandwich).

Soon, the singing,
songs that hold you,
each one an enchanted world
as you walk out one May morning
or with that foundered ship
the Mary Ellen Rose
you rise again.

Then, the dancing!
Such moving together
with a partner, with a set,
the whole ceilidh-ful
thrumming
one heart, one rhythm.

In that moment
you are called home,
you've come home.

A simple chorus moves you
rolling home, rolling home
and while the ballad lasts
grief is made lyrical
the ordinary, blessed
laughter reconciles
strangers are well-wishers
and painful differences
harmonise.

You know it has to end
(Adieu, sweet lovely Nancy).
The bright tented city
like a sepia Midsummer Fair
fades, is folded away.

The Monday workaday world
is raining greys
but the folktune
you find yourself humming
is a rainbow in a green garden.

Six Poems from "A Welter of Days"
(Outpost Publications 1977)

A Lull in March

A lull in March brings the quiet waves slapping
at the salt-scoured shingle on the empty shore
and the brown young herring gulls glide in the water
which is glimmering with dreams in a soft yellow haze.

Go, love, go now, before the summer evenings
stretch and diminish in a welter of days;
soon come the mad winds, hurtling to certainty,
and memory will falsify what it cannot restore.

When my children are asleep

If, when you wake, you find the spring
  has turned to summer, you are no more child
    and I am gone, then do not cry;
      I could not wish a better waking.
For you must live, I will not tell you how.
  Yet, when they say the world is sick, why bother,
    friends are broken, parents in the grave,
      I will not tell you how, but
but there is an end to sorrow.

I could wish you'll hear the music
  strange and high close to the stars;
find, though night is cold about you,
  some friends never turn away.
Some say dawn can hold no promise;
  still, it is another day.

If you break your heart for joy
  I shall never quarrel with you;
if in love you mock the winter
  I need never tell you how,
and if self-disgust should blight you
  still I will not tell you how –
but, when everything is empty
  when you cry no more, no more!
and death seems the only answer
  then I'll whisper, oh my child,
    though I do not know quite how
there is an end to sorrow.

Dark Mercy

Through fear of action and mistaken action
where all decision cannot help but tear
the living tissues of a twisted love
a final blunder tips the circumstance;
then in the mind the whole conundrum turns
begins to spin, to whirl, and sight goes out.

Whose are the warm arms holding me?
  Who put this pillow at my head?
Who feeds me? Holds the cup for me?
  By whose hands am I gently led?

Mercy is dark and full of angry words.
I thought it was despair, that bitter salt
which stung, which blinded, and which battered me –
thought I was drowning; in a sea of love.

The Dreams Lie Dustily

The clocks wind down, the dreams lie dustily,
and only gulls in Hastings are awake.
We sit and drink and talk till half past three.

Afternoon town of pensioners and tea
where pampered ducks doze on the sleek park lake
and clocks wind down and dreams lie dustily.

Even the young aren't stirred up easily.
Why get so fussed? A fuss is all you make.
Just sit and talk and sleep till half past three.

Up at St.Helen's, bowed bare heads agree –
such worthy pains the undertakers take
while clocks wind down, and dreams lie dustily.

Whatever's done, they'll call for you and me,
so let the pictures close, the stucco flake;
sit down, and we can talk till after three.

Urgent, the grey-humped thrusting of the sea;
to blame a place, a parasite's mistake:
the clocks wind down, the dreams lie dustily
because we merely talk till half past three.

Thirty

Receptivity declines; friends talk now
more of mellowing than of change.

The powerblind politician in the skull
barks out his blank imperatives:
Habit-formed centres of decision-making
delegate immediately to dormant abilities!
Should I join his muster
for bigger and better
drum myself fervently towards
some dark dynamic animus?

Resolutions come in
and go out with the new year
observes experience, which promises
to compensate for slackening drive
by a dexterous marshalling of resources.

The more I can explain the way things are
the less able I am to alter them –
techniques of avoidance
without skills of discovery.
Where experience suffered a setback
it has come to a standstill
and quietly entrenched itself
building a house of serviceable responses.
I potter about inside
and don't go out much.

Thirty is the time
for a series of deplorable disturbances
in one's most respectable suburban areas.

The War
(Lahore 1971)

When first I heard the guns, I ran.
The students in the hostel cheered
and roared Crush India! Pakistan Zindabad!
When the jets thundered they shook their fists
and stood on rooftops howling God is Great!
One wept for joy. Jehad.

And in the hush between the sirens
we waited, asking if it came next time
it should come quickly;
the crows in the pepul tree at night
clucking and cawing – could they hear
what we could not? – and Shammi
bringing chrysanthemums and talking
about rolling bandages.
If we should go, she and Saleem, betrayed:
and should we stay, people at home in pain.

And when we told him, Saleem wrote:
"I never knew chrysanthemums had claws
or that the blood could cry
that autumn caused the flesh to fall away
and leave the bones shivering and surprised."

Now we are leaving, such little armour
as I have mustered against what I know of death
is so much air, a few small words
lost in the shaking of the earth
which somewhere, now, as the sound dies,
brings a silence.

Desert and Courtyard

Sand scours the baked earth mile upon barren mile.
Harsh rocks glare. Eddies of hot air whirl dust in swaying columns
like desiccated genii dancing with the skeletons of thorny scrub
on the corpse beneath the mirage: the wispy, withered memory of water.

Build high stone walls
round fragile and brief lives.
In the shelter and shade
allow the filtered light
to paint mosaics
on the jasmine
and the lemon trees.
Fountain is the heart
of the courtyard garden;
chiselled marble panels
gleam geometrical.
Place silk cushions in the alcoves.
Rest. Listen to the plashing water
while the muezzin calls the soul
to evening contemplation.

Time cools and slows.

Qanawat Temple
(Damascus, Syria)

Another Constantine conversion job:
the ruined church hallows a Roman temple
in an Islamic land.
Black basalt columns exhale an oven heat
on chattering, deciduous visitors.
What's that by the wall?
A litter of black smudges.
Mulberries! So ripe the merest touch
brings a bruise of blood.
We laugh. Our Hammer Horror hands
run with the sweet, rich, purple juice.

Up at the apse
a great ridged altar stone
used to catch the blood
of slaughtered animals.
A shudder like distant thunder
silences our laughter.
Across two thousand years
ghosts have stroked our hands
with memories of sacrifice.
Did the Byzantines preserve this holy table
to hallow the earlier lambs of god?

Our hands are witnesses: blood still haunts
the troubled earth beneath the mulberry tree.

A Nile Journey

Coarse sand blows across cracked lips,
jumble of crumbling mud walls, the desert
always at the end of the street.
Mustafa comes into the cramped back yard
to wash, limbs suddenly sleek, shining
like polished granite, eyes of a Nile god.
He strides away, blood beating to a pulse
unbroken since the pharaohs.

In the night of a valley tomb
an adamantine figure, chrysolite eyes wide open,
echoes the living step. Desiccated power
moves left foot forward over the threshold
into the after– life. Four millennia later
tourist courtiers in trousers and trainers
gawp at the boy king's chairs and thrones.
His murdered eyes stare down the sunlit Nile

where cruise ships dispense milky tea
to pale Europeans, gazing at tall–masted feluccas
and the dusk trees crowded with white birds.
Beyond the dark groves of palms, the broken rocks
of the desert valley tumble closer.
A sphinx murmurs:
liquid eyes turn to crystal.
Make love on this rich river.

The Spice that is Morocco

Rashid of the Blue Turban
(heartbeat, drumbeat of Africa)
kissed us in the night street
gave us sunflower seeds
and said he loved us.
A true Tuareg welcome.

Not like cucumber England
affluent, technical, dull green –
no, here's smouldering Fes
heaving in pungent medieval seethe
tradesmen ragged but smiling
abundantly social, familial
while we have lost fellowship
to interminable emails.

Flocks of black plastic bags
flap like crows, roost dustily
in the thorn bushes. Soaring above,
the red rocks of El Rachidia radiate,
marbled with miraculous green;
down in the valley floor, parasols of palmeries
date, fig, olive, almond, pomegranate...

This is the story of Morocco, red and green
elemental as the High Atlas
fierce and gentle, hot chillies, mint tea
honey transfusing the soul,
the spice that is Morocco.

Seeing Through
(for Judith Everitt)

"Every so often
you see right through
and the world
comes round to listen," you said.

You see through
egos with their
murmuration
of twittering emotions

you see past
the animated foreground
of the day's chores
and scuttled encounters

see the smiling light
in the cradled face
light playing in the eyes
of children wading the water meadows

or you see the shadows
of the drifting past
silting up the soul
scarcely struggling.

What can you do
Inbetweentimes?
Scholars study,
fathers bedad;

you can try to be yourself
in saint-like dedication
aspiring to authenticity
through the waiting days

but the occasional spell
a cheeky push of your will
may just summon the messenger,
open the unexpected window

so, banish the mornings of soap and anguish
walk past the doors that tell the same tale
wish for the seeing, the right word, the path
through the maze, round the corner

into the amphitheatre.

Dream and Daylight

Daylight seeped down
into my dream.

It was my seaside town
but my house had gone;
they were my friends
but they were forlorn.
I was in Nick's basement
with discarded chairs and doors.

I went downstairs in the daylight
for a cup of tea and toast.
It was my house
but the wistful dream
kept welling up.
They were my friends
but their time had gone.
In the basement of my mind
the old town was forlorn
still existing, but abandoned
and my seaside home had gone.

Underneath the comfort
of my breakfast cup of tea
and the welcome of this daylight
lies the old town by the sea,
discarded doors, detritus:
the old dream that was me.

Paper Boat

My old home has broken up.
The floors were slack,
the good wine gone musty.

Now my car is a boat
between islands – a college,
a class, a concert:
a bright anchorage
is a meal in the cottage,
a little houseboat, cooking
in the low-roofed galley
hoping the floor will stabilize
beneath me. A conversation,
a hug, then the night passage,
the alarm and mystery of dreams.

In the car I talk to myself
between lives, casting around,
lighthousing ahead. A sudden lurch
down a wave-cliff, comes fear –
is there strength in my arms to row?

So I turn to the paper boat of poetry
to navigate, make a structure;
find some new sufficient metaphors.

My boat casts a shadow
like a dim island on the seabed –
another life, moving
over the fossil-fractured floor,
nosing for a landfall
where boat and shadow touch.

Find the current,
steer for the amicable shore.

Sleep

This song, a summoner:

Come evening, may the day have been
a plain green June, your thoughts
quite trite; then, when the inevitable moon
begins to draw the sun's levelling light
to its silver crescent cradle

your long shadow may be full of mystery
not fumbling fear, and as your shape
darkens to indigo, see, see
the glimmering, navigational stars
and tomorrow be as coloured as you please
once sleep, that quiet and sliding ferryman
has rowed you over the night lake
with breathing strokes.

Oh may no old sore jib you
work tension churn you, no
nor personal discord distress you,
no-one, none, and nothing more
than sleep's night summer soothing air
enter your mild mind.

Sleep.

Mousediary : Midwinter

An unexpected joy today –
they brought the bread with bits in.
Ah, malted grains! Cheekpouch–filling,
whiskertwitchingly good.

And a great terror. The young giant
brought in two other young giants
and they kicked the skirtingboard
till I thought the dust would choke us all.
They are incomprehensible!
They love the snow.
Today they were excited
as they were the first to cross
a whole field of it, those
paw-freezing acres of winter desolation.
Mind you, underneath the snow arches
can be fun... but not a patch
on being the first to cross
a pale gold pat of fresh unsalted butter.

Tomorrow we commemorate
the gods of milk and mould
who married to make glorious cheese.
And Tuesday it's the feastday
of Esmerelda Divamouse
whose shriek–squeak of a high C
could stop a rampant tomcat
dead (I hope) in his tracks.

So I give thanks, this night, great Soulmouse,
for being heart whole and home
with a chocolate shortbread
and the merry mouslings
mewling contentedly.

Candlemouse, from my high street chambers
in the seventh litter of my mousefulness.

Steeple Woods
St. Ives, Cornwall

Struggle
up to Knill's Steeple.
Atlantic sleet
stinging steelpins
icy javelins.
The Monument
a storm blasted mast,
unreachable horizon.
Wind slaps you
stone cold.

Hurry down
to the woods

and shelter.
Drifts of brown beech leaves
cushion your footfall.
Quiet here under the gusts.
Ancient trees whisper
in the eerie dusk light.

Boulders heave up
thick felt skins of moss
oddly lit
as if moving
like shoulders, great elbows
pushing through
sudden rushing of leaves...

They ARE moving!

Hurry home.

Emma, sheep dog

Collie girl, Cornish maidy
playful, neat
light, springing paws
to bound up with nip-and-lick
a yip of greeting

tail a feathered brush
sweeping delicately
soft white-and-tan coat
to roll in badgercrap
with a twinkling, white-lashed eye

then lithe and away
head down low, fast so fast
a soul sprinting, an angel
laughing, a pulse
of life itself, barking

adventure!

Lawn, Normandy, June

"Sh! They're coming. Marguerite,
stop nodding at Mireille,
you'll weaken your stem.
Madaleine! Another twirl from you
and the mowman will get you.
Eh bien, here we go –

DAISY!"

And as we walk onto the lawn
white swirls unfurl in the sunlight
pale paisley–patterned flags
settlements, towns, whole cities
daisies pacquerettes daisies
rampant, rolling, a summerful,
a triumph of daisies.

Dusk. Delicate mauve–pink fingers
curl over tiny yellow heads –
thousands of frail little foetuses;
and as night settles
the lawn is a troubled dream
shot with frissons of fright –
the mower! The mower! –
white pulses and surges spiralling
through the galaxy of daisies.

How could we? Nonetheless
we trundle out the mower guillotine
and white heads roll in swathes.

A green silence.

"Pssst! They've gone. You there, Monique?
Félicitations, chérie – you helped
to mangle the mower.
Mimi! Put your petals straight.
You are NOT dying of consumption
in a Paris attic, but yes
you can lead us when we sing.
Ready? Grand ensemble –

DAISY!"

Coltsfoot

Post-war bomb site.
London. February.
Ghosts of dead willowherb
blanched, sunk in corners.

A child, alone
under the bare bushes
haunted by some trouble
trifling matter for adults
but blown like a wrecking storm
through a child's world.

I crawled gritty on all fours
through that desolate heritage.
Then coltsfoot, shining,
startling yellow, alive
sea anemones in a magic pool
fringes of fresh, transparent yellow
looking up at the grey sky.

The air smelled sweet.

When I walk back
through my life, and at fifty
taste that implacable February,
I do not take with me
a philosophy of redemption
but I hold a small,
fierce yellow hope:
coltsfoot again.

Isle of Mull

Shattered fish boxes from Mallaig and Glasgow
scatter the tide line, bleached as bones;
human wreckage which the grey rocks spurn.
Black boulders, lumps of jagged coke,
sit rooted in memories of molten heat
ignoring the navy of the sea, which boils emerald
and spits raw foam, leaving these rocks
bright with igneous shine.

A lifespan is an eyeblink here
where Ardnamurchan scans the Sound of Mull
and the blunted backs of Eigg and Rum
jetty the further Cuillens of Skye.
Far across the sharp blue line
of unimpedable Atlantic, outer islands
Barra and South Uist, rival the clouds
beyond the crouching shores of Coll
then vanish in a moment's mist.

Our eyes urgently reach for them
as boundary stones; if they are there
the ocean and the sky beyond are anchored:
we have respite from whelming winds
and cliffs of encroaching rain.

Fairweather townsfolk, we have names
for what we see here, but the glens
and rocks remain intractable. We pass on.
The kittiwakes wheel, veer off and cry wild;
their calls are absorbed, and die
in the silence of a cold volcanic sleep.

The Wind in the Long Grass

Once, at night, I saw the moon
erupting from a storm-torn, sea-wild sky,
and there, beyond the path, the field rolled down
as if it were the heave of a green wave,
and opposite me on the valley's rise
there stood a man whose eyes I could not see,
his face moon pale, his hands half raised
with open palms towards me.

If it was to bless,
it was a stroke I could bear once only,
as the whole hill
the wind exulting down its switchback slope
was tumbling in a rush towards him,
and all my startled senses longed to dive
down that green gulf and up into those arms.

The moon
melted, and the wind
sighed as if a sudden force
had broken through the hillside
and was gone, gone to a place
I could not go

and quieted, became a land-sweet breeze
sad, but sad
with all the softness of satiety,
and I was left to walk the darkened path
alone.

Since then, each time
the wind stirs the long grass
I wonder where that sovereign master goes.

Seadream

The colder, sharpening salt of the sea
cuts into the last bouquet
of summer in the air.
Warmth still lingers
under the promenade wall

where I stand.
Vast water under open sky
makes changes in the seasons
merely ripples; waves constantly
disintegrating
silver-grey like dreams:
sea-drift, dissolving
the where and what I am,
absorbing the foetal self
into sea, only sea, primordial sea.

The great derivator
heaving with its own slow seethe
breeding, indifferent merely
to humans who have grown away.

Yet it draws us,
induces us.
Am I contemplating the sea
or is the sea
subconsciously
gestatingly
dreaming me?

Sylvia Plath
(The Arrival of the Bee Box)

She claps, slowly. Even the high cirrus
hurtle in anvils, the wind gusts
in greenhouse February, the thin sun
is tortured to a sick silver.

I told you so, Plath crackles
in awry, dry Maine, as we abuse
our earth, begin to blame ourselves.
She always knew we were hell.

Gaia, in your name, can we
open her bee box and become
the blossom that survives the stinging storm,
her rage, your rage, her words

a lash, a loving legacy?

August

Sovereign summer
sun decrees
southern days
and golden ease.

Morning glory
one day long
fills all August
with its song:

"Blue serene
mauve star
cloudless heaven
trumpet flower;

Lovers never,
never part
in the sunwarmed core
of my honeyed heart."

Capri

The black bees of Capri
harvest the sea's blue in their wings;
secrets shine
in their dangerous silhouettes.

Morning glories, whole walls
of wild, violet blue
throb with the touch
of the night goddess.

A strong, bronze swimmer
dares the sea's turquoise boil;
siren rocks shatter his life
with a little shrug.

The style, the nonchalance
of Capri's gods and emperors!
Over the blue of Naples Bay
the hunched shoulder of Vesuvius

mimics the imperial innocence:
who, me?

CYCLADES DAYS

Breakfast

in a lemon grove
spears of light
fierce spots of energy
dance on the dazzling tablecloth
whitewashed visitors
startled, alarmed, enthralled
seek out the little chairs, Minoan blue
under the bougainvillea balconies

honey spreads its warm sunlight
over cream of yoghurt
cinnamon biscuits, hole-in-the-centre
crunch with sesame seeds

slender cat stares silently
great wide ears, pointed dignity
ancestry of Mother Egypt close by
one moment soft and playful
next, cousin of the tiger
scornful of lumbering humans
spurns the offered yoghurt
but is avid for butter
(feeding the kittens)
you must not notice her need
but cat-like, look down your nose
respect the intensity of her desire

and find yourself lapping your coffee

Morning

Fish silver the surface, make spirals
reflected on the white hulls of boats
in the curved harbours of Naoussa.
The fort is a cut-off tower
thick walls, crouch-low arches
like a pirate stronghold;
boys leap up the rocky, crumbling stair
the rigging of their ship
doom their mates to walk the plank
and plunge into the waves below.

The islands are ships, only anchored,
capable of slipping their moorings
and stealing up, clear and close in sunglare
or floating away in duskhaze, deceptive,
dangerous even, voyaging.

The bow-wave from the chugging ferry
makes whole rainbows, leaping like dolphins
over the living blue of Aegean water.
Up in Ancient Thera
a carved dolphin still leaps
but only in the high meltemi wind
while the dry old gods
on Mount Profitas Ilias disdain:
move on, ephemeral mortal
your human eyes
will only see this moment clearly
when you leave it.

Midday

Gritty field
grass is straw
earth hot dust
heat white heat
god–fierce threat
colours drain
body sags
pouring sweat.

Red and black, the rocks of Santorini
remember the volcanic heat
molten layers metamorphose
beneath the quartz–white houses, cubes
perched like nesting seabirds
on the cliff-rim of the caldera.

(the lightest of clothes
chafe with the sandpaper
of unwanted intimacy)

Seek the shade of Antiparos cave.
Invasive tourists have broken off the stalactites
warm air and human touch
have dried out the mystery
cool depths of rock now colourless
the reverent silence dissipated.

In the zenith sun
eyes mere slits in a vizard.
The body commands:
fear Apollo, find shadow
cease any movement
retire, retire; leave, leave
the god to gaze upon a marble wreck
his native Delos, sacred lake drained dry

Afternoon

waking in the underwater cave of the white room
white-blue glowing, restful water-blue on white
fresh air drowsiness, heatweight
lifting in a light breeze

then the benison of water
the body wriggling like a child's
with the cool pleasure of it
alive, at ease, at peace

on the beach, each pebble
is a marble carbuncle
clear, bright water, jade green
deepens to electric blue
the sky above pale, powdery
over the still-quivering khaki
of the conical mountains

the whole sea confident, primal
liquid lapis lazuli

Evening

Beneath the small blue dome of Ageos Andreas
old islanders gather on the terrace to talk
and watch the sun's fireball set
a serene legend of majesty.
Inside the church
little stars of candlelight
float on the cooking oil
a sympathetic magic
invoking the feint stars
in the vast milky-blue dome above.

No sadness at this sunset,
at this parting.
This light is not to be diminished
extinguished by grey Gatwick
or insipid English tea.

There is a godlike summer certainty
to the rhythm of these days.
The daily returning sun
awakens some inner eye
gleams out from the Aegean
vibrating
as if the waters themselves
were the source of the numinous blue.

This light of the Cyclades
gift of Apollo
glimmers within,
illuminates the journey.

Elderflower Champagne

A green but desolate place. I was a child
caught for seven summers in an ancient domain
of farm-bound powers. Oak and mayflower,
ash trees and bracken, spilled their shadows on the dark
private intensities of that time, where wild
elderflowers fermented champagne.

The taste startles the memory. Like champagne
it effervesces with the past distilled. A child
smells ice cream in the early dew. Boys, wild
with catapults and rivalries, hold the domain,
and whispered terrors in the candle dark
echo until the nightmares flicker and flower.

My aunt alone could exorcise them. Flower
she did despite the mudsea farm. Champagne
she was against my uncle's dark,
irascible moods. He roared at cows, a child
throwing stones to hurt, tormented in that domain,
bullish and lost. The war had driven him wild.

What could a mind like hers do but go wild?
Alone; regrets. (Ah, Meistersinger, an elderflower!
I should have married Walter.) Yet the doldrum domain
of W.I. teas fizzed full of chuckles as champagne
when she burlesqued them. And a child
could rest at home in her rich, breathing dark.

Once back in London, school, a different dark,
struggling with textbooks, rules, and wild
desires and disappointments. No more child,
I lost her mystery, which could make dreams flower,
and floundered in fantasy. Later, brut champagne
was glamorous; shadowy: the adult domain.

Now with her death I see the whole domain.
Too late to tell her that I know how dark
that desert farm was, what bright champagne
her yeast and honey made there, and how wild
with weeping laughter she made me. One elderflower
stark on her grave: the mute love of a spell-bound child.

Farewell aunt, and flotsam child. Adieu, domain
of heady flowers, that opal life, now dark
but wild with vintages of elderflower champagne.

High Summer

At the bend in the lane
a wall of wheat.

The dark green of the wood
slopes off, heavy with August
as if alarmed
by this dust-gold barrier.
You are alone, quite alone
when the moment of high summer hits.

An absence of friends, parents, children –
there's a gap,
a not unwelcome sense of emptiness,
of freedom, even;
they have all slipped away
into their separate summers.

The wall of wheat
stuns, arrests, mesmerizes
in the heat, the breath-holding quiet.
Your body is at ease, yet troubled
by a whisper, a sistrum of fear
at this force, this majesty of wheat,
this fortification of summer.

The urgency of spring trails far behind,
the coolth of autumn
no more than a ripening blackberry,
leaving you suspended
in the sunlit silence
poised, alone

at the fulcrum of summer.

The World for his Pleasure

News bulletins twitch
with the might and muscle of the States.
And here he is, Mr America, on a Thai beach.
Young man, 27, divorced, tattooed,
would like to meet unwilling world for profit.

Logistics company, Baghdad. Fifteen Americans,
four hundred Kurdish guards. Next month, Dafur.
He lives in Kuwait in a secure compound,
makes money enough to retire at forty.

Civilised, our conversation, but
I have to challenge American policy.
He is courteous, intelligent; suggests
possible benefits.

Trekking in the Himalayas, diving in the Red Sea –
his National Geographic enthusiasm has the energy
of the American Dream, and I am an old Briton
spectator now, envious even, and can only nod

as he strides to his kayak, and waves,
turning lives to gold and ash in his salute.

Landscape, Seascape

Mistletoe runs riot in the Normandy apple trees,
a thousand dandelion sunclocks
pixilate the fresh green rush of the grass.

Look at all this life
says the insinuating voice of death.
It all goes on without you.
A snowfall of cherry blossom shivers the spring,
the tight buds clench with the amber of autumn.

But the sweet moment of now
the birdsong, the soft dance of the trees
wires up to the memory

of an evening sea glide on a Thai beach,
guarded by gigantic karsts of orange limestone.
Megalithic precipices of glowing rock
gaze down on the long-tail boats
skimming and fracturing
the sun's low golden track,
rainbow scarves waving on their high prows.

It is all still there without us
and yes, Death,
it will still be there
when we are gone

but the red and gold glory of it
shoots through the speedwell blue
of this northern sky.
The memory and the now
fuse.

Death pales, rebuked,
and must wait.

At Seventy

My skull echoes, reverberates
the wave-wash of memories
all those departed days

distant now, whispering
a life previously seen
through stained glass windows

kaleidoscopes

fragments still glow
mysterious as Chartres
prismatic elusive possibilities

only a perspective
remote as the stars
suggests a pattern

Mahé, Seychelles

Perfection.
Why does it make me
think of death?

Here, the Indian Ocean
inspires its dawn miracle
the birth of colour
sapphire and aquamarine
below the world-rim
of blue-tempered steel.

This is a light to lighten February.
It rolls across huge granite boulders
the petrified giant tortoises
of Gondwanaland
while the limpid sea makes love
to the blue pipefish, lulled
in a womb like coconut milk.

Primal palms, a forest
of coco de mer three storeys high
sway, a sound of drumsticks
rattling and clacking
subsiding to a Jurassic silence.
A world of unstained green before the Fall –
there is no irony in Eden.

This is how I should like to die:
to sigh with the receding surf
as the Southern Cross emerges
from the indigo sky
and dissolve into ocean
under the circling stars.

ACKNOWLEDGEMENTS

Some of these poems originally appeared in
New Statesman, New Poetry, Outposts, The English Tradition
Christian, Country Quest, Trinity Review etc.

Thanks to Roger Dunkley for his close reading
and encouragement, and to my son Andrew (Moose)
for his technical help.